Beg No Pardon

Also by Lynne Thompson

Through a Window, 2005 (chapbook)

We Arrive by Accumulation, 2002 (chapbook)

Beg No Pardon

LYNNE THOMPSON

PERUGIA PRESS
FLORENCE, MASSACHUSETTS
2007

Perugia Press extends deeply felt thanks to the many individuals whose generosity made the publication of *Beg No Pardon* possible. Perugia Press is a tax-exempt, nonprofit 501(c)(3) corporation publishing first and second books by women. To make a tax-deductible donation, please contact us directly or visit our Web site.

Cover image is *Ringshout, 1999–2000,* a 120″ × 120″ watercolor by Richard Yarde, used with permission of the artist. Yarde's conception of the body as a self-healing organism has shaped *Ringshout,* which takes its name and inspiration from a religious ceremony and healing ritual performed by African Americans during the slave era.

Book design by Jeff Potter and Susan Kan. Author photo by Leroy Hamilton.

Library of Congress Cataloging-in-Publication Data

Thompson, Lynne, 1951-

　Beg no pardon / Lynne Thompson.

　　p. cm.

　ISBN 978-0-9794582-0-0 (alk. paper)

　I. Title.

　PS3620.H6836B44 2007

　811'.6--dc22

　　　　　　　　　　2007013099

Perugia Press

P.O. Box 60364

Florence, MA 01062

info@perugiapress.com

http://www.perugiapress.com

I have brought my witness eye with me
and my two wild hands . . . .
— Lucille Clifton

CONTENTS

Three

THE POET, APPLYING FOR A JOB, CITES HER PREVIOUS EXPERIENCE

as a witness. Passionate secret.
Collection of colors, rubbish,
pins, puddles, buttons, paper,
detritus to scrape, to paint,
to polish. Conjurer of mummery
and feral thought. Flotilla
of aberrations. Eccentric drop
of ink. Gnome on a trapeze.
Inclination. Hand drum. *Obligato.*
Vertigoed butterfly. Professional
sphinx. Silence. Sizzling arrow.

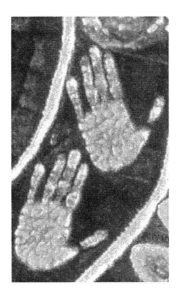

One

Where are my ancestors buried?
In the feathers of a yellow bird.

How do you remember me?
As seven wishes.

Where will I find the shape-changers' magic?
In fields of hydrangea.

Who teaches your tantara?
A fox behind closed doors.

Where are your elephant birds?
In ruby and absinthe afternoons.

And where is the sawfish beak?
In the dayshine of trees.

How deep is your river Betsiboka?
Twelve earthquakes deep.

What time did your soil turn red?
When calves bent their knees . . . .

IMPERFECT GHAZAL FOR AN UNKNOWN MOTHER

Because memory lives beyond death,
you're still weeping for me.

Because guilt's the eternal hammer,
you're still bruising banjos for me.

Because my bones were carved from yours,
you're a rug of broken mussels for me.

My songs are flat and coarse
because you're walking south from me.

Because my name was never my own,
your choice has been a prison for me.

Though I weep having seen my death,
you are still living for me.

SHE, NAMED P_____ AT BIRTH,
SPEAKS TO ME, SAYS

"You think you know who you are;
you do not. You think everything's great
in your gravy train life, your feet up
on the taboret, sipping fingers of Pernod
and blowing smoky O's of Gauloise
like you were born to it. You were not.

You were born at County Gen., the random
upshot of a collision between an urgent
virgin, a married man, and the backseat
of a Studebaker though everyone knows
there was no joy the night you got made.
You came into this world on cotton rough

from 10,000 washings. The doc showed up
late, then spilled a little Maxwell House
on the sheets; the nurses yawned. Mama cried
for you for sixteen hours before her water broke
and she's been in labor for you all her life. But
no one came; no one came to see. So in time,

mama just gave you away. Of course,
you don't remember that just like you don't
remember me. Me, who never got the pretty
dresses. Never got the vacations at the beach.
Never sat down with the family to eat lamb
and mint jelly on a sunny Easter day. No,

you don't remember me. It's as though you
were born to the manor, born to speak lousy

French and read Edwardian novels in a hot-
house, to gad about at high-tone schools,
to raise your finger just so, so the ruby shines.
But you don't know who you really are, Miss

Don't-Remind-Me, Miss Given-Away-Four-
Times-Until-You-Were-Taken-For-Good. Well,
you got my blood in your veins and you ain't
no fancy dancer, you ain't no pearls and piety,
you ain't no seashell by the seashore, and you
sure ain't no evening out at Lincoln Center.

You got me in your veins, got my chipped white
fence, my regular job, my 39-dollar-a-night
room in Vegas, and this name that ain't gonna be
at the end of any poem. But don't worry, my sister,
my slip of a pen, I'll never let you forget the night
you were born, my name was all you had."

How I Learned Where We Come From

When she wants him for the late meal, she calls
supper soon Kingstown-man, curried goat, sticky-wicket

and he responds, testy, *not yet ready, Bequia-woman,*
Anglican church, basket with no handles.

We children, we laugh, head for the hills
and the tall sweet-grasses, listen for the lilt

of frangipani tantie. She call *come in now*
pigeon peas, mangoes, poor man's orchids —

then we run, for true, and supper is all
cassava root, callaloo, very little sugar cane

and we're in it all at once: choirsong above
Mt. Pleasant, Port Elizabeth, harp of Paget Farm

till Father, he say *no,* defends his slipped-on wishes
for Soufrière, Sans Souci, Wallilabou Bay

and so on into the evening, calypso and steel drums,
a little Rasta and Bob Marley for us young'uns

until, finally, we are no longer black ironwood —
wood that will not float.

SEED OF MANGO, SEED OF MAIZE

I saw one of the grandmothers only once
in a photograph.
Short and sturdy she was, a black black Carib
with a forehead wide as the sea
that kisses Port Elizabeth
and a nose broad as the nostrum of Admiralty Bay.
Breathing deeply,
her breath was fume of coconut and allspice,
mango and frangipani,
black bird and blue sky,
was the isle of Bequia.
She conjured a daughter,
then jinxed another,
and they bedeviled five daughters between them,
and I am one of those flying fish.

The other grandmother I composed from myth
and half-told stories.
She was a red red Cheyenne —
scorched earth,
much chased —
sported a thick reed of braid
pulled off from her forehead,
wide as Dakota
before it was north and south.
She hisses warnings across ten, then ten times
ten more years to a son
who reshapes them for me
in my dreams, sometimes in my waking.
As flute, blue maize, dance of the sun, she comes,
crow on the wing, singing up the ghosts,
and I am one of those — a ghost, singing.

A Found Art Between Razors and the Blues

The trick that fooled me was She brought me home —
She brought me home when home was already full
of testosterone
but She wanted ribbons and I wanted ribbons
so we all had a good laugh and when I was looking
another way
She shoved pins
and needles
and razors
and swords
and carving knives
and tin cans
and Her fingernail shavings
down my throat
and snakes

      and shadows

          and bile and seaweed

               multiplied

in my throat
and I became afraid:
the hair on my arms turned into gnats
my eyes bulged like a gargoyle's
if there was a god, he made my blood flow forever for no good reason
and my head became a TNT factory
my feet endlessly mired in a lonely muck
and every flower that can ever be known shriveled
in my hands

and my hands composed onlythebluesonlythebluesonlytheblues
(and did I tell you that She killed something once?)
and I became afraid
and fear shrouded over
and it rained on and it blew through and it danced around
like an old Negro caricature and that was the trick
that fooled me and I thought *this will last as long as it lasts*
like a wake of vultures
or a pile of millenniums:
the T'ang Dynasty
the Catholic Church
the Ming Dynasty
the War of the Roses
the Middle Passage
the War of 1812
the war against prohibition
and everyone denying
every woman
has a right

but She died

        and died again

and she kept on dying

while her tricks faded —

till my eyes
found their place
in my head

Pinkie's Father

Mr. Jackson doesn't have to work. He's a full-time lover, a honey man who spends his time applying Madame C. J. Walker's hair pomade. He's taken to being entertained by long-legged women who stop by to pay their respects for his lost missus about the time we come home for Cokes and Fritos after school. We take turns peeking at the women, admiring themselves in the long mirror down the hall, *after*; laughing and slowly applying shiny red lipstick, examining their teeth and straightening their hose, looking like they know what makes a Chevy's engine work. Passing us by, they smell like sweet gardenia, rose, or magnolia mixed up with some unidentifiable smell that drifts out of Mr. Jackson's bedroom. There, we sometimes find small, empty boxes, the kind lined in satin and made to hold men's gold-and-silver cuff links. Dreamy music blows from the hi-fidelity player in the parlor — music like Garner's *Misty* or Duke's *Mood Indigo*. Mr. Jackson looks at Pinkie and me absent-mindedly like he forgot we *always* come home at 3:30. But Pinkie and I gotta jitterbug and rock 'n roll, teach each other how to put on Maybelline's *Moroccan Red* lipstick and admire each other and ourselves in Pinkie's yellow bedroom mirror for hours and hours —

DADDY TOOLKIT

His favorite child was the garage where
he dissolved into nail, screw, nut, and bolt;
where he became the personalities of a
wrench: combination, adjustable, chain.
On Saturdays, he reigned in his kingdom:
master of sledgehammers and mallets.
He ruled there as hex-nut driver, push-
drill. When Mom called him to supper,

he'd turn winch, vise, ripping bar.
When I begged him to stay, he'd whisper
in my ear: *a plane is a tool used to smooth
the surface of wood* and *an adze is used
for chipping and slicing.* Most important
of all, *steelyards use balances and counter-
balances.* I loved knowing he'd always be
my ladder jack. I loved learning everything
I would ever need to know about men.

JOE

Saturday mornings, Mom's sport was laundry — sopping white
sheets wrapped 'round her till she wrung then flung them

like clouds while Daddy stretched out under the hood
of our old Chevrolet.   My brothers disappeared, so I did too —

over the low brick wall and through the high hedges to Joe,
still wearing his robe after 10 A.M., two bowls of Wheaties, sugar

and sweet cream at the ready, Motorola tuned to *Road Runner,*
and after, *Scooby-Doo.* I didn't ask *what happened to the money,*

*Joe? Is it true your Daddy Barrow was a share-croppin' man who
died in a nuthouse?* No one mentioned Schmelling or the Brown

Bomber, Rocky M or punch drunk. The only smack we heard
was lips on spoons, the only crunch, toasted wheat.

BACK SEAT

Long before I learned life repeats like an unchecked burp,
I was a schoolgirl sitting in the last seat of a yellow bus facing
backward like I'd been told more than one hundred times
not to do. It was raining in that all-at-sea way it used to rain
in southern California before there were so many cars but
even then, there were too many. And the street was Adams or
Pico or some other familiar street although here, the familiar
is always being knocked down to make way for the unfamiliar.

One day, there was a blue & white car with sharky fins and Cheerio
tires following very close to the bus and every time the bus stopped,
those blue & white fins stopped too and just missed us by inches
and I thought *that car sure wants to hit us* (as though a Chevy has a will
of its own) until it did and I went flying — Peanut's lunch pail, satchel,
and all my golden pencils spilled like pick-up sticks and my bottom lip
split on the silver grab-on rail like a spoiled banana and it's been that way
ever since: collisions, broken bodies and nothing, nothing to be done.

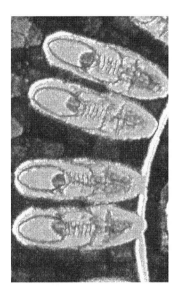

Two

FEAR OF THE BIT

First came a fear of pronouns, under-
pants, tin. Next, she noticed her parents
feared evolution and abstract paintings.
They taught her to fear one-liners, drywall,
and the entire state of Georgia. She taught
herself to fear receptacles, sportscasters,
corkscrews, and the number nine. While
others admit to a fear of interbreeding
and nomads, a clan of wild gypsies fears
Big Ben. Some Christians own up to a fear
of the Jews. She's even heard that race-
horses have an understandable fear
of the bit. Her firstborn — a sweet, smart
thing — says he's learned to fear statuary
but his sister declares that she fears fear.

I was a skinny novice utterly lacking in any technique other than
Comic Book/Missionary/Spread Eagle when I took a lover.
His hands and hips had been scarred by fire and, for some time,
his pin-wheeled skin held me as spellbound as the lovemaking.
He'd learned to live with it since swallowing the most quixotic

of childhood's bitter memos. But it was grisly news for a wide-
eyed sugar tit who'd only fielded a few minor assignations, all
with those smooth-talking juvenilia so eager to scramble onto
new opportunities. But his buckled flesh called for something
young colts don't always give up to the tether — tenderness,

a startled tenderness that is sparked by communion between
souls as well as bodies. It rushed from my fingertips onto his
headlands once fanned by flames that came dangerously
close to his right to replicate himself; that seared his tissue into
the color of days-old death (gray, ashen) or the crumbly color

of Central Avenue. Even after so long, his hardened skin held
the flavor of charred hides and changed into different patterns,
depending upon the light, much like sand when it swirls across
the Kalahari. He hustled my curiosity for all it was worth.
He knew it would gentle me, teach me how to light the flame.

SHORT STACK WITH SWITCH MONKEY

I'm a free wheel. Got no one telling me the can or can't do.
So when this jeans-too-tight-to-breathe strolled into Miz
Willie's Grill, I liked the cut of his kerchief right off. Knew
he knew things I wouldn't know in a lifetime: how to bail
it in, strut in company jewelry, and play the glory hunter.
That's why I wanted him. Him straddled out at counter's end,
nursing a cup o' joe hotter than Yuma's breath, looking neither
left nor right, just talking to Miz Willie who didn't look left
nor right or give a damn about anything he said. But I did.

So I sidled up to the counter, took the stool two stools away
and bought another cup while I listened to him blow smoke.
Listened to his world of slow train, hotshot, piggy-back. Heard
how he would catch out ahead of the bull, drug runners, and
ramblers with romance in mind, trying to follow him out past
San Berdu, all the way to Baxter Springs. Listened long enough
to know he'd never tie on to a can or can't do or to me. Finished
my cup o' mud and lit out — full on a cheap pie card, a rail fan
looking for a local load, all smiles from a stack of short love.

THE HOUSE OF MANY PLEASURES

It never matters what time it is
in Rampart's House of Many Pleasures
'cause there's always a scent of incense
between the hours of bourbon and no-goods.

In the violet dusk, some cool papas with coin
are always sniffing after us;
they beg us to low-tone their bugles, slide
their water keys, to shake our castanets.

In the scarlet A.M., some used-to-be-some-
body's-mama always shows up asking
after her Tom, Dick, or Harry, all the while
memorizing the scent of our brass.

But we're no *diminuendos* and we cannot
be riffed. There is no other, no *Skylark* nor
Sweet Lorraine. We're the blues the world
forgets when we lie between a man's thighs,

perfume of sin and reefer bleeding
from our fingertips. We are wildcats
for a sweet daddy. We bite when you beg us.
Here, in this Sidney Bechet dark, this fugue

for the hardcore, we slide bronze and wet
from Louis' horn at half-past dreams
in this House of Lethal Delights where
you tell us your tawdry secrets no matter

what time the violet dusk, the scarlet A.M.;
where we taste of cinnamon, taste of clove
about the time we surrender,
about the time we slide you down, *slow* —

ELEGY FOR THE RED DRESS

Good morning, Red Dress,
double strand of pearls, faded rose
perfume clinging to the bodice,
the slip, the silk of the sleeve;
molten to my hips, my breasts,
the drum of my heart, hem
softly pleated to a permanent party.

Hello and hey there, Red Dress —
heavy with the sweat
of *Love Wants to Dance.* Scented
with hopes of Shy Man, Bold Man,
Begged-to-take-you-home Man.
Still crumply down the back
from the hanker in their hands.

Highway 61 Blues

you begin with a sound wrapped around a syllable . . . .
— Quincy Troupe

Woncha take me Bobby J? Woncha take me
up the trail outta New Orleans, past Natchez,
past Vicksburg, all the way to Rollin' Fork?
You and me gonna beat the boll weevil,

gonna beat the bent back heat all the way
to Duncan, all the way to New Africa been
on my mind. I'm lookin' for a blue devil,
a blue devil to set me free from floodplains,

from Yazoo, from Tallahatchie, fly free me
all the way to Greenville, Tutwiler, all the way
to Clarksdale where my guitar just gotta moan
Preachin' Blue all the way, all the way, all the way

and I'm hollerin' loud *I been 'buked and scorned*
Willie Brown; I been beat down Howlin' Wolf;
hey Kid Bailey, got any scratch? Can you get me
to Shelby where blues ain't dead? So said some

pretty one-eyed gal who gave me two six stringers
and a hard drum, said *pace yourself, pace yourself*
and yeah, Mr. Jimmie Cotton soothe me sure with
some sweet, sweet devil music to keep me movin'

outta sullen heat and deep blue and
Jim Crow and sharecrop — no mo' dry throat,
no mo' hot whip, no mammy sold to don't know
where, no white man's cotton but no forty acres

and no goddamned mule, *yeah,* so take me, Bobby J,
all the way to Memphis, out west to Houston,
up east to Cincinnati, up north to Chi-town, away
from the woncha please *Stop Breakin' Down Blues.*

THE UNWORSHIPPED WOMAN

Nothing
              beat her

break her down or   reek so
          the way she do

nothing got her unzipped mind
              her fly-paper memory

she a riverbed   will be
for a dog's millennium

                    she gone lost
to her un-borns   she pale smoke

shadow   *in the distance*

              she a train whistler's whistle
      this unworshipped   this   woman

she come like salt lick   she go down
like a drowning man hollering for one last last

her story hung like seaweed

                    she come in   she go out

      like unworshipped women   supposed to

              knees bloody
                    knuckles got somebody's

jawbone jammed on

        hair coiled with September twatterlight
        corkscrewed so tight even owls won't hoot

until   she pass by them   longing, on long legs

        lips the color of peril

bittersweet   folded round a hollow in her twisted back

    But   her one good eye   it flash —

GIVE ME THAT RAG-BAG RELIGION

1.

The world is a ragbag; the world
Is full of heathens who haven't seen the light;
Do it, Mr. Missionary.

2.

God's neon advertisement: *The sermon this morning*
will be "Jesus Walks on Water." The sermon tonight:
"Searching for Jesus." It's miracles in the A.M.
gone to crap by o' dark-thirty. Any congregation
that understands that is just the place for me.
Check out Sunday night's bulletin: *The Church*
will host an evening of fine dining,
superb entertainment and gracious hostility.

In another: *Don't let worry kill you —*
let the church help. Finally, someone is listening!

Even listening when I come to sing:
The senior choir invites any member of the
congregation who enjoys sinning to join the choir.
I tell them I'm an alto and always in demand.

So, 3.

I've found my holy temple. The king of kings,
his minions, and all their silly pastimes
designed to return me to the fold,
devised to aggravate my faith:
The Associate Minister has unveiled
the church's new tithing plan —
I've already upped my pledge, now up yours.

SOAR

No one ever said *housemaid* or *domestic*. Pride matters more
and here's the truth of it: she was *Tantie,* a grand-mothering

substitute chained to Miss B, a former Hollywood come-hither
and Tantie's final misery. I couldn't name a single movie Miss B

had starred in but Mother told us she was a first-class bitch.
Thirty years later, watching late night television, I recalled:

I met that bitch once. Ill-preserved on celluloid, she fluttered there
amidst her ersatz brood — but not in the same way I'd seen her

flutter decrees upon my tantie. And my tantie, once a muck-a-muck
in her own right (having flown an airplane solo in days when

most women and Negroes were grounded), half-fluttered in return —
to make sure her family had dimes and nickels. Tantie didn't tell us

she was Miss B's maid, and I never knew a thing about it until I saw
this black-and-white movie with Miss B — half a star among stars —

given third-place billing — nearly unrecognizable as the cold shrew
I remembered flaunting dipped pearls, telling me to

look and admire because I would never own anything
quite like them. Tantie calmly laced Miss B's tea (with what? —

we never knew) so that Miss B napped a little longer on afternoons
when Tantie fed us sugar-cubes, spoke softly of days when she soared.

SONG FOR TWO IMMIGRANTS

I thought I knew you. To me, you were the Grenadines,
the Anglican Church, and a cricket match every Sunday,
and every Sunday, you were Fort Charlotte, the Vincy Mas,
and blue tide pools. You were Arawaks sailing into Kingston
Harbor. You were English and French patois, rainforests,
regatta and a Congo snake, whelk, *rotis,* lobster, and rum.

Yet, here you are in a yellowing photograph, in the Mojave or
Death Valley, C A, looking like deserters from an American war:
her, every bit the boy, hair slicked, leather jacket cinched at her
throat, her tiny foot on the running board of a black '37 Ford
coupe — and you, looking nothing less than the black Clyde Barrow,
flicking the butt of your Lucky Strike, checking out your boys
at play in the dirt wearing short pants and high-tops — everyone
looking for all the world as if the Caribbean was a dream, a far
yesterday away, and it was, and it's clear I did not know you.

HALF-BROTHER HOLLER

I hear you been looking for my daddy —
I hear you telling everyone who'll listen he fouled
    your mother and she got you —
I hear you say you don't want no trouble
    but you troubling the water, I say —
I say *why* and *what you want* and I ain't heard
    no good reason — no good reason after all
    these years — no — you just wanna kill my momma,
    my boy and girl and for no good reason 'cepting
    I just wanna know —
and that ain't no good reason to trouble the dead —
'cause dead is what is and where he be now
so — you just go and tell his dust 'cause dust
is where *you-mean-nothin'-to-me* can be found.

RAFFIA

To the Igbo, everything is family, everything
is connected, Grandmother explained.
Like the weave of this raffia hat, we intertwine.
See? This is the world to the Igbo.

— Chris Abani

To the Igbo, everything is family, everything —
be it small or grand. Whether you look like
I do or look otherwise; whether you can sing
or have no voice at all. In all of nature — moon
fish, elephant tusks, the silkworm and its
kin — no essential distinctions
can be made. Those who discriminate bring
dishonor to our house, perpetuate the shame
we never want to admit. When singled out,
we wilt needlessly. Relatively speaking, everyone

is connected, Grandmother explained.
We bleed the blood of both aborigine
and Inca. Our imagination doesn't strain
under ice-plains or inside the heat of the Gobi
or any other desert at the thought we all
advance, slow as turtles, but we advance as one.
(And those who cannot, must be saved like grains
of rice fallen from the rice-pot. When we refuse,
we're doomed to sever the natural connection
that makes us humane and proves that

like the weave of this raffia hat, we intertwine —
the lock of your blond hair braided with my
dark lock, your breathing identical to mine.)
Where is there a line separating the clouds
showering our cities? Even the caesura

between twilight and nightshade can't be
assigned with precision. All of history is a sign
that we learn and fail and fail again at the very
same rate. That I hold the tether and decide each
bend in the path your sheep will take. Don't you

see? This is the world to the Igbo.
To think otherwise is to dwell in double doubt.
To live otherwise is to live where there is no
point in leaving your tent. This is not difficult.
This won't fill your basket with kolanut. This
is a story to be read by us all every day. We all
have a grandmother who's confirmed it, so you
cannot say it isn't so. Some young Igbo from
a tribe near your village are awaiting your call.
Their breath is indistinguishable from yours.

SMALL, MAD PLANETS

We are all small, mad planets —
our veins swollen and sock-eye red,
memories short and less than useful;
they cannibalize our bloodstreams.

Old folks, knotted, gnarled, will tell you:
we are all small, mad planets, no less
twisted into a hump-backed tango,
no less implanted in this sad magenta soil.

Perhaps our batteries are dead or our
smoke alarms can't recite their hard luck
and so we become small, mad planets
where rain in Djibouti doesn't matter

any more than snow piling up in Duluth.
A child's creaky yellow wagon is stilled
while a woodpecker's rap is hysterical
because we're all such small, mad planets.

Rapid Eye Movement

While I am sleeping, I am many different things —
much more than just couscous or rum whiskey.

Only last night, I was a fur ball but usually I'm
not even from this country so time travel isn't

a problem. Listen you smarmy heathens, you don't
have to build a better breast for love to come on

full throttle. Just hide your mismatched socks, tooth
decay, and terror, and *please, please* don't wake me.

come to me in the swagger of night.
Whether you are struggling vampire
or foe or star-breath, come — oh yes —
when I am in the land of malfunction
and curious syntax, of Strayhorn played

on Saturn's rims, come, when late-light
is least opaque. When owls start their
hooting, come. Whether or not I agree,
come like you've come on no Saturday
night before and alone, or, if you must,

come with your hands full of thyme.
Stay until the metronome stops then start
that tango all over again. If you come
to me, I'll give you lusty pandemonium
because, after heat-hard hours, I become

most true. Before it is too late — (and
isn't it always much too late?) — come.
And when we are completely filled with
the rue of our felonies, of our fallibilities,
tide and turn, then come once more.

Jazz

I've lost the abracadabra in my right eye.
So introduce me — casually — as a man;
perhaps he'll know how it is love heals.

But for people like me, it's improvisation
that balms the scar tissue, bisects twilight
and the usual gin fizz and every pale

moon that stipples this hard, white land.
I swear by skins' players who thread day
and the dog with delicacy, embroider

with their holy heat. But some bells keep
up their clanking, welt-deep in the flesh,
stutter, like a Jesus speaking in tongues.

TO BLACKNESS

As it happens, I have never tired of blackness — its Marcus Garvey,
Raisin in the Sun, Tuskegee airmen. Its Strivers Row and liver lips;

its Dred Scott, Freedman's Bureau, Scott Joplin. Some say black is
swarthy, gloomy, evil, fiendish, but we all spring from the tribes —

Ashanti, Bobo, Fulani, Wolof — their cowrie shells and krobo beads
sewn into our fading fabric. I don't know much about my native blackness;

my daddy he say *Igbo,* the only word he can give me, but it's the only word
I need to get the old folks to remembering that in Igbo *ututu* is morning,

abali is night, and in any mirror, my *ihu* — my face — is always black.

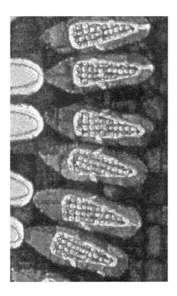

Three

Playing the Dozens

> *But each of us*
> *deserves, in a reasonable life,*
> *at least a dozen times when death*
> *doesn't take us.*
> — Lawrence Raab

The first was on the frenzied voyage
through the birth canal.

And when, without permission,
they gave her quietly away.

At her first grade feeling-up by Diego
DeJesus while flying on a swing

and when blessèd blood pooled deep
then spit its prayers down her legs.

Then later when castanets rattled
in her father's throat and chest and

the day her heart broke into thirds
and fourths and fifths then dust.

One brutal December at the Dakota
when a Beatle vanished in the brume

and the day that all her prayers fell
still before her babes could be born.

Once there was a girl who ate paper but not just any paper — no Macy's receipts or mattress tags. No, she preferred Proust for breakfast, a little Tolstoy on toast. During school recesses, she was seen gnawing on *The Weary Blues.* Always bored by just one thing, she devoted the seasons to variety: Shakespeare in spring, of course, and always, always, Pushkin in December, every other year. Every other year, she left luck to chance. In '92, the holidays were all James' — Henry, Joyce, and Baldwin. The family was a little put out by it. Harrumphs and tongues clacking were heard across the dinner table. In photos, her image looked like *The Color Purple's* Celie. All she knew was that everything on earth was a-bristle. One year, she disappeared altogether. There's even a tale (tall-in-the-telling we're sure) that when she finally took a merchant for a lover, she hid *Sonnets to Orpheus* beneath his pillow which he tolerated until he found *Death of a Salesman* atop the tank of the john and fled. Recently, she was spotted in serene repose on a California beach, a tattered copy of *The Myth of Sisyphus* clutched between her teeth.

LIP OF THE WORLD

You may think you want to die —
your best lover leaves,
cool cash comes up short

and god is living in another state.
But you do not or even if you do,
your calves and thighs, heart and

breasts and sinew do not. Once,
in the Grand Canyon's belly, I learned
this lesson. One mile down as the crow

flies but for seven switched-back miles —
all vertical — I was sure I was a goner.
I couldn't think of family or tomorrow

or that yesterday, life had been easy-go
and a fish fry. But I looked up and there
was the lip of the world and I grabbed on.

PAS DE DEUX

At their steel sink, peeling Idaho potatoes'
dirty brown gowns, feet at rest in an odd
position, anticipating the *battement tendu,*

she remembers him and their daughters who
wait; bids *adieu* to the shadow who bows for *bon
chance,* head to kneecaps, twirls off, stage right.

MARRIAGE, A FUGUE

Which naked body
is yours?
You were salt
at breakfast
but by cocktails,
your asters
were in bloom.
Your spine is a
bow for a cello
but still
I know you
as betrayal.
I'm lost as a girl
but hallowed
be my ova,
hallowed
be my tongue,
hallowed be
the soles of my feet
but halleluiah
you're a stranger.
Call me
when the cycle's over.

Canvas Reluctant to Become
Joan Miró's *Dog Barking at the Moon*

I've been standing in this corner for a while now,
smile taut as a stretched cloth can be, and I know
what's going on — I see what you've done to others.
I've seen *The Tilled Fields* with a whole world
watching — eyes everywhere, ears in the locust trees —
and I know you are watching me: eyes, ideas, and
contradictions a royal flush for your mind.
On the canvas across the room, *This Is the Color of
My Dreams* waits to be sold, your words writ in
black, indelible ink. What will you write in your
notebook for me? A toenail? A crescent moon?
In the light that dawns before the light that is day,

you choose brushes and I am born from the shapes
you find in cracks in the walls, in the ceiling.
I am born, but not before the red and gold ladder
that leans on nothing, goes nowhere, reaches for
a star that stars in no galaxy. Not before a far planet
dances with a Checkerspot Butterfly glad to be done
with its migration. Not before the moon that wanes
with a cherry on its cheek or before your sky
and earth have grown black and brown with the for-
getting of themselves, the forgetting of everything
they've been led to believe was true. Not before I am,
finally, dog with a lemon for a mouth, wistful in white
spats and blue nylons. Not before the last layer of paint
on this immortal comic strip or one last yap at the sky.

SCISSORS

There's no synonym
for scissors. Everyone
with a Roget's knows that.
Rock. Paper. Scissors.
And by *cut*, of course,
you may mean *score, sever,*
abscind, dissect, disjoin, cleave,
but scissors are instruments
unto themselves. Just like
you won't find a synonym
for Utah or any other state.
Many things just can't be
said any other way: toothache
or mercurochrome or 1951.
So, when I say *it's over*, I don't
mean *interlude* or *maybe.*

CRESCENT

What today is like
is unlike any other thing
that ever will be.
The saucer will never again
hold its cup at just this angle.
A shadow that's begun to wane
will continue to fade forever.
A baby, seeing her brother
for the first time,
will never again see him
for the first time;
he is going out the door.
This should make you
neither happy nor sad;
this is what makes you.

QUICKSAND

May held on for a long time but that's over.
Even in the backwash, there are no answers
and you're a fool if you think so. It's all
shifting shorelines and sinkholes now. Yet,
it's okay you say; you're a trumpet lamp
with a handmade shade; you're a thousand
costumes with matching shoes. And love?
You're its darling dumpling pot sticker!

How sad. Watching you run around,
lost, with no papers. You will never return
to the home you once knew. Oh, maybe
some dog walker will hire you to tame fleas.
But look what you're holding in your lap —
surly October — and you don't even know it.

COME BACK, MISTER SCISSORHANDS

Kim: Hold me. *Edward:* I can't.
— Edward Scissorhands

In my dreams, his name is Hunger Unspoken. His name
is House Still Sleeping, is Cigarette, Wolf, and Cold Coffee.

Under my lids, his name cascades like snow,
slips away like black jade, one minute *paraìso*

then suddenly *cara-de-cão* or *ninho des vespas*
and I am as old as I am. In my useless reveries,

I speak more softly than the dying
when I call to him: *night horn? root of a scream?*

It's then I know him as bliss, thin air, a cock-and-bull story,
as Johnnie Lace-Up.

He has lived with me, without ceremony, until he is, as he is
always, *gone* —

CURVES. *RAPTURE.*

Loved ones,
    as I write,
    I succumb
    because,
    as it turns out,
    I was never well.

How surprised
    you all can't be
    knowing that I,
    a woman,
    black-hipped
    and single-living
    in Los Angeles,
    put my trust
    in Levi Strauss.

You tried
    to warn me:
    drink less gin,
    wear light clothing,
    tune out.
    I didn't listen.
    When I did,
    I couldn't hear.

Quacks prescribed
    musk oil and bustiers.
    Both failed
    so it's come to this:
    Lynne, a desk, a pencil.

Roget on a romp —
rapture is
to killjoy as kindle
is to regret as
John Ashberry is
to Jean-Michel Basquiat.

Y mirá. El duende
está en amor con
mi iPod que ame
negative capability
and the slender curve
of a comma —
its stiletto stuck
in my throat.

Thirst

or in old English, *thurst* — not just a desire
to drink, but to yearn. Medically speaking,
polydipsia, desire to drink in the extreme
which happens when one has been too long

parched. So butterfly kiss me. Or haven't you
ever seen a daisy, head of petals bent, ready to
join the mulch heap just past sunset, brought back
to sanguine stem by morning dew, glistening?

SIDEWINDER

Post-menses arrived drenched in the sweat of a woman
who will never have children: moist accusation

dances above the fat curve of upper lip — birds bathe
in her underarm pits spit near a brand new mole.

Nights are lilac and wild. Nightmares are something
of a pimp and burnt aftertaste of ash lounges

on her tongue. Rainwater smells coppery, then limp
roses dumped in a witch's wheelbarrow. Sauntering's

not difficult but a triathlon is a lousy project
if she wants to avoid the vapors. There is banter

all around — pure nonsense and overhead, there's a side-
winder in mourning skid. She may be a mud-stuck,

carbine woman no longer capable, hands full of stinging
jalapeños, but why are there no shingles of regret?

BALLAD FOR YESTERDAYS

Buzzing like a hawk over high
cotton — in a trance — I saw you

where human lust is electrical, all
gyration and heartbreak, a July'd

moon and sun. Drowsy with beauty,
we spooned in sweet, fallow fields so

which of us is more mad? (Or is this
melancholy just a corn cob dipped

in red roux?) Still, we were lovebirds.
Perhaps we invented our own jazz;

sweets, we were mornings' glitter.
And yes, there were afternoons of scat,

of bee-bop. But there is no loving that
won't splinter from itself and we know

time is just a honey dripper. Yet, I'm all
dreams and hunger all these years later.

A Persistence of Gravity

: you come out swinging your sickle
cut down the tall sward
plant the seeds
then wait for the seasons to do your bidding
but you are not in charge
and tempests will come
or drought
or a retort of locusts and all things will die
so you drop your lure into lakes
and your bait is the best of the very best ones
and you have biblical patience
believe every perch and trout
is eager to latch on to your enchanting line
don't know they're happy a-swirl in their watery worlds
because you are not in charge
and all you can catch is the rubbish and dross
other anglers have dropped
so you strap on your power
blast off seeking Neptune's Dark Spot
a colony where you can hoist your flag
but you are not in charge and when you race home
the same old attacks, counter-attacks, and crossed swords,
beggary, starvation, and even greater butchery
that you are complicit in
but you don't want your children to learn of your crimes
so you bury your face in your wife's bent elbow
hide your hands behind your husband's warped spine
glad they will comfort you
more glad they'll tell you lies
which is why you can pretend to live in smug quarters

and it will go on like this for a time you cannot predict
and it will go on like this until you turn over
on the bitter sheets of your daybed, stunned, and then :

I am Grenadine

having been born of elite black masses.

I am a slaver washed up on Spring.

I am Lower Bay and its blackbird.

I am the great-grand-niece of Chatoyer;
chipped fretwork on his chattel-house.

I am sharpening stones from Queensbury;
mist sheltering sugar plantations at Farm,
a dwelling house joined to the cane,
to the windmills, to the waterwheels,

a hodgepodge of Karaÿbe footnotes
in Father Breton's diary; he say —
    from the very beginning, they were
    filled with hatred, not just for slavery,
    but any form of injunction, authority
    or submission…

This is why I run to the sea.
    Being well-supplied with rivers,
    I oscillate windward and leeward,
    dangle a bracelet of fishing cays,
    tattoo of Bordel petroglyphs
    on each palm, Yambou Pass carving
    the bones where my elbows curve.

In 1780, I was harried by hurricanes,
under heavy fire from all enemies.

But I stride with considerable numbers —
led the insurrection at the Massarica River.

Some say I am one-half Anglican Church,
but I am thorny and cut down.

I am never six furlongs from Kingstown.
There, I am after-ash of Soufrière, 1902 —
or so my daddy tells —
all internal wars,
pregnant with destruction,
fled in different directions.

                    Today,

I am golden guava, Young Island, Grenadine,
and my name will not be confused or improved.

BRUISED

pregnant with grenades —
wrong-eyed pinball —
barely a heyday —
                        yet
poet-she — gap chronicler —
colloquial sponge — *gin spill*
                laced through ink—

always, she returns
to a theater of degree
and faraway diction

imagine — can you? —
a more subversive magnet —
a silkier wound than this —

this sandstone requiem —
this dirty-yellow moon?

A Sorceress Strolls New Grass

I am neither mother nor turquoise neckwear
but you are such young women,
such new potatoes, and there is much
for me to tell you:

    that bishops joyride in the dead of night,
    that blue's favorite color is blue
    and earth is just a gaudy paragraph.

And though I am ripe as November, I can tell you

    no sorceress ever abandons midday
    and a sculptor is always better
    in a waterbed.

Of course, I'm vainglorious with my knowing and croaking —

but you women are writing your own Book of Migration
and without warning, I feel useless as an empty valise.
What you know makes the bandicoot fly and you converse
in flamingo and seashell, smell like smoke and rapscallions.

    You are tambourines
    in the stewing pot,
    a crucible of cymbals.

    Being fresh as new grass, you
    inspire me to astonish, then gloat;
    to beg no pardon, then begin.

NOTES

The epigraph for the book is from the poem "the killing of the trees," copyright © 1991 by Lucille Clifton. Reprinted from *Quilting* with the permission of BOA Editions, Ltd., Brockport, NY.

"I Ask the Malagasy" refers to the people native to the island of Madagascar.

"Short Stack with Switch Monkey": *Switch monkey* refers to a switchman on a railroad.

"The House of Many Pleasures" was inspired by William Pajaud's painting *Rampart Street Ladies*. Mr. Pajaud is an African American artist living in Los Angeles whose art reflects his Louisiana roots.

"Highway 61 Blues": The epigraph is from "Words That Build Bridges Toward a New Tongue," copyright © 1999 by Quincy Troupe. Reprinted from *Choruses* with the permission of Coffee House Press, Minneapolis, MN. The reference to "Bobby J" is to legendary bluesman, Robert Johnson.

"Give Me That Rag-Bag Religion": The first stanza is from "Sporting Beasley," copyright © 1989 by Sterling A. Brown. Reprinted from *The Collected Poems of Sterling A. Brown,* ed. Michael S. Harper, with the permission of Harper Collins Publishers, Inc., New York, NY.

"Raffia": The epigraph and the first line of each stanza are from "Geography Lesson," copyright © 2004 by Chris Abani. Reprinted from *Dog Woman* with the permission of Red Hen Press, Granada Hills, CA.

"Jazz": The second line is a variation on the first line of "Unnatural State of the Unicorn," copyright © 2001 by Yusef Komunyakaa. Reprinted from *Pleasure Dome: New and Collected Poems* with the permission of Wesleyan University Press, Middletown, CT.

"Playing the Dozens": The epigraph is from "Permanence," copyright © 2000 by Lawrence Raab. Reprinted from *The Probable World* with the permission of Penguin, a division of Penguin Group (USA) Inc.

"Come Back, Mr. Scissorhands": The Portuguese words translate as "paradise," "dog face," and "wasp nest."

"Curves. *Rapture*.": The Spanish can be loosely translated as "And look. Deep soul is in love with my iPod which loves . . . ."

ACKNOWLEDGMENTS

The author gratefully acknowledges and thanks the following publications and Web sites where versions of these poems previously appeared:

Blue Arc West: An Anthology of California Poets: "Scissors"

Cider Press Review: "Imperfect Ghazal for an Unknown Mother"; "A Sorceress Strolls New Grass"

Crab Orchard Review: "Song for Two Immigrants"

Eclipse: "Curves. Rapture."

Indiana Review: "How I Learned Where We Come From" (also appeared on Poetry Daily)

Masterpieces of African American Art/An African American Perspective: "The House of Many Pleasures"

Pearl: "The Poet, Applying for a Job, Cites Her Previous Experience"

PoemMemoirStory (PMS): "Marriage, A Fugue"; "Quicksand"

Rattle: "Playing the Dozens"

Runes: "A Found Art Between Razors and the Blues"; "Raffia"

So Luminous the Wildflowers: An Anthology of California Poets: "Seed of Mango, Seed of Maize" (also appeared on Drylongso. com)

Threecandles.org: "Fear of the Bit"; "Rapid Eye Movement"

Writersatwork.com: "Canvas Reluctant to Become Joan Miró's *Dog Barking at the Moon*"

Yalobusha Review: "Pinkie's Father"

ABOUT THE AUTHOR

Lynne Thompson was born and raised in Los Angeles, California, by parents born in the Windward Islands, West Indies. She received her B.A. from Scripps College and a J.D. from Southwestern University School of Law. She currently serves as the Director of Employee and Labor Relations at the University of California, Los Angeles. An active member of the Los Angeles literary scene and a Pushcart Prize nominee, her poetry has been widely published and anthologized.

In memoriam, mothers of my mothers —

Ida, Cleopatra, Mary

ABOUT PERUGIA PRESS

Perugia Press publishes one collection of poetry each year, by a woman at the beginning of her publishing career. Our mission is to produce beautiful books that interest long-time readers of poetry and welcome those new to poetry. We also aim to celebrate and promote poetry whenever we can, and to keep the cultural discussion of poetry inclusive.

Also from Perugia Press:
- *Lamb,* Frannie Lindsay
- *The Disappearing Letters,* Carol Edelstein
- *Kettle Bottom,* Diane Gilliam Fisher
- *Seamless,* Linda Tomol Pennisi
- *Red,* Melanie Braverman
- *A Wound On Stone,* Faye George
- *The Work of Hands,* Catherine Anderson
- *Reach,* Janet E. Aalfs
- *Impulse to Fly,* Almitra David
- *Finding the Bear,* Gail Thomas

This book was typeset in Sabon, a family of oldstyle serif faces designed by German teacher, calligrapher, book designer, and type designer Jan Tschichold (1902–1974) as a homage to the 16th-century work of pioneering typefounder Claude Garamond. Tschichold based the italic typefaces in the Sabon family on the letterforms of Garamond's contemporary, Robert Granjon. The type family, designed to accommodate the technical requirements of a wide range of hot metal composition equipment, was released from 1964 to 1967.

Type on the cover and section divider pages is set in Joe Hand 3, a calligraphic font by Dutch illustrator and painter Jeroen Van Der Ham. Van Der Ham's digital type foundry, JoeBob Graphics, released Joe Hand 3 in 2006.